ALLUSIVE
POEMS

ALLUSIVE POEMS

CONTENTS

CONTENTS

ACKNOWLEDGEMENTS

Thank you to God for the creative ideas.
Thank you to my mother and father, brothers and sister, wife and child for the love and support. Thank you to all friends & people that have taken an interest in my work keep sharing, liking and supporting to help.

Thank you to James Keith Burley for the front- cover design.

OTHER WORKS BY THE AUTHOR

"Escaping the poverty cycle" available in E-book format. About some financial and other considerations I wish I would have thought about whilst young to better myself and others.

SYNOPSIS

This book is a collection of poetry that has been made by myself and kept for years the earliest being 2009. I have waited so long to build a large enough collection and be able to distribute in a format that it deserves. The inspiration for these poems is life in general at times of great emotion or at night I would wake up and write or sometimes one line of a poem would run around in my head until I put it down on paper or until I wrote the rest of the lines to finish it. I hope you enjoy it as much as I do.

SMALL BOX

I have failed to fit in your ideal box or pigeon hole

I guess for this someone else shall pay my toll

Maybe one day people will stop to see

Ask themselves why does it always have to be about me?

Even the ones you love find it hard to share

Thinking that you should always be there

But this is a human's greatest fallacy

Believing you will be the one person to live throughout history

But like everything else we all turn to dust

Nature guarantees this is always a must

So just like how you judge me and want to fuss

Nature is there to take care of all of us.

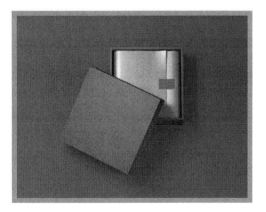

SMALL BOX ANALYSIS

I have failed to fit in your ideal box or pigeon hole

Sometimes we do not please people and have wanted particular circumstances to occur in our life (job & finances)

I guess for this someone else shall pay my toll

Someone else will be looked upon to please them by doing what they require

Maybe one day people will stop to see

Ask themselves why it always has to be about me?

Our need to get people to do what we want them to is greed and self-serving

Even the ones you love find it hard to share

Sometimes people do not involve you by telling you their emotions

Thinking that you should always be there

People take it for granted that they can always use your ear to influence you

But this is a human's greatest fallacy

Believing you will be the one person to live throughout history

But like everything else we all turn to dust

Nature guarantees this is always a must

We can't be around to please people all the time eventually we have our own lives to fulfill and live out

So just like how you judge me and want to fuss

Nature is there to take care of all of us.

Regardless of peoples wants and needs we all only have limited time

PEOPLE

Ever stared at a spot so long it turned black

Ever realise the only way to sleep is on your back

Then when you awake your surprised

Because you cannot remember when you closed your eyes

All you know is the system shut down

Whether or not there were people around

But in the morning it will restart

With the pounding thud of a heart

Although it has been beating all night long

Your mind was not conscious until the dawn

Up and about to carry out some routine

The, only way to avoid is to live out a dream

But this does not happen for all,

We can be six feet but still very small.

Live out life always lacking one thing

But then when you have it, it does not make you sing

It leads you to see there are greater priorities to be sought

None of them at a price that can be bought

Is this about life, death or imagery?

No just simple poetry!

Take from this poem whatever you want

But leave some for me because it is not about your want

Or need not about money not about greed

But simply said it jumps from a to b

To talk about life's history.

PEOPLE ANALYSIS

Ever stared at a spot so long it turned black

Sometimes we can focus on things so much we fall asleep or our vision blurs

Ever realise the only way to sleep is on your back

on your back everything is aligned such as your head and neck but on the side
you can have poor circulation with organs strained

Then when you awake your surprised
Because you cannot remember when you closed your eyes

Sometimes we fall asleep and do not remember when and we are surprised how little
or long we slept for

All you know is the system shut down
Whether or not there were people around

Sometimes you can fall asleep with noise or people around dependent on how tired
you are

But in the morning it will restart
With the pounding thud of a heart
Although it has been beating all night long
Your mind was not conscious until the dawn
You are not aware of your body's functions in the sense that you do not control your

heart beat telling it to beat but it operates by itself
Up and about to carry out some routine
The, only way to avoid is to live out a dream
Most of us do a job like a routine from 9am-5pm

it seems like the only way to avoid this is by thinking what you would like
to be doing (daydreaming)

But this does not happen for all,
We can be six feet but still very small.

Sometimes we have what we think we need (education or money) but still do not get
fulfillment

Live out life always lacking one thing
But then when you have it, it does not make you sing
It leads you to see there are greater priorities to be sought
None of them at a price that can be bought

As humans we always feel we are missing one thing even though we could have so much

Is this about life, death or imagery?
No just simple poetry!
Take from this poem whatever you want
But leave some for me because it is not about your want
Or need not about money not about greed
But simply said it jumps from a to b
To talk about life's history.

This poem can mean whatever you interpret it to mean.

NATURE

Opinions are sought to categorize me

This is a humans' highest priority

It started off with the colour of the skin then how many pounds you can collect

All this just to gain some respect?

Don't try and preach or tell me of your hate

If you wanted me to care it's a bit too late.

I did care once when your opinion mattered

Now if I look your way you should feel flattered

There is only so much a body can take before it has to go to mend

And you cease even being considered a friend

It may seem cold well then I am below zero

I have given up my job I am a retired hero.

NATURE ANALYSIS

Opinions are sought to categorise me

People are always judging trying to put you in a category

This is a humans' highest priority
It started off with the colour of the skin then how many pounds you can collect
all this just to gain some respect?

History has taught us people are always looking to differentiate and discriminate against people for different reasons

Don't try and preach or tell me of your hate
If you wanted me to care it's a bit too late.

People try to influence you with their concerns that are negative

I did care once when your opinion mattered

Sometimes we can go from respecting people highly to not respecting them after we see their bias or hatred

Now if I look your way you should feel flattered

Sometimes we cut off negative ties

There is only so much a body can take before it has to go to mend
And you cease even being considered a friend

For our own good we have to keep away from hearing or being involved in too many negative situations

It may seem cold well then I am below zero
I have given up my job I am a retired hero.

The position I used to fill of listening to hate or biased is no longer mine because I do not stay around to listen

ELECTRONIC EYES (WRITTEN 14.08.09)

Walking along,

The road is not mine,

drop any litter and I will face a fine for the roads I pay to be swept.

So the road must be kept clear at all times

Except for traffic and kids committing crimes.

Flip this round and look from my angle

how life is becoming much more of a strangle

Deluded or not I will chase that carrot until it's mine

or at least till I run out of time

But many more can see just like me

that it is becoming old and stale, but weak and frail

they will try till they prevail

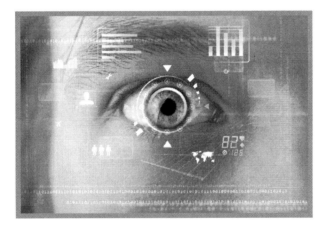

ELECTRONIC EYES ANALYSIS

Walking along,
The road is not mine,
drop any litter and I will face a fine for the roads I pay to be swept.

*I do not own the road but neither does the government and our taxes pay for the
roads to be swept but if you drop litter you could face a fine*

So the road must be kept clear at all times
Except for traffic and kids committing crimes.

*There's an irony in how rules are made to stop litter being dropped yet crimes could be
stopped and aren't focused on as much*

Flip this round and look from my angle
how life is becoming much more of a strangle

*with allot of new laws we face the erosion of our rights leading us to feel pressurized
like we cannot do much without being in trouble*

Deluded or not I will chase that carrot until it's mine
or at least till I run out of time

we all try to get what we consider an ideal life and chase this dream until our last day

But many more can see just like me
that it is becoming old and stale, but weak and frail
they will try till they prevail

*even though we know it is just a carrot on a stick we still chase
it believing we can have an ideal life*

UNDER THE SUN (WRITTEN 19.08.09)

The time will come when all men shall be one under the sun.

When people agree they are tired of war when disease stops and there is no more poor

I can see it in my thoughts are you there with me yet?

If not you could be the biggest threat

Unable to see what is destined to come

When men shall be equal under the sun

When all your rewards shall be shown thus far

This doesn't just mean a house and a car

Or maybe you're in debt not the recession kind

But the one where you have given up all hope in your mind

stopped the wonder of what you could do

and are just trying to see things through

should we be open to look to the sky?

wonder when? How? possibly why?

UNDER THE SUN

The time will come when all men shall be one under the sun.
When people agree they are tired of war when disease stops and there is no more poor

most religions believe that eventually there will be heaven on Earth

I can see it in my thoughts are you there with me yet?
If not you could be the biggest threat

If people can't imagine ever living in peace it is dangerous because they may be used to war and problems

Unable to see what is destined to come
When men shall be equal under the sun
When all your rewards shall be shown thus far
This doesn't just mean a house and a car

It is believed you are judged for your time on Earth and rewarded accordingly

Or maybe you're in debt not the recession kind
But the one where you have given up all hope in your mind

You may not be in financial worries but you are in trouble if your mind has given up on the idea of peace

stopped the wonder of what you could do
and are just trying to see things through

people sometimes give up on their dreams and just go day by day not really living life but become like a robot

should we be open to look to the sky?
wonder when? How? Possibly why?

Should we consider there is something higher than us more knowledgeable than us? that can bring peace on Earth when the time is right

IS LOVE NOT? (WRITTEN 24.08.09)

Is love not knowing what you love about them?

Is it not knowing what you would do without them?

Is love right for all or just some?

Does love make you want to run?

For joy or fear we try to make it last

Try to put bad things in the past

Since love forgives all and is such a sought after gift

But love is all we have so let's take care of it.

Like a drug you want to sustain

because when it's over you're left with pain

it may take a toll on your body every time it fades away

often leaving you balding thinning or grey

IS LOVE NOT?

Is love not knowing what you love about them?
Is it not knowing what you would do without them?

Questions the reader as to what they think love is, can it be subjective or objective?

Is love right for all or just some?

Not everyone agrees with marriage or believes in love

Does love make you want to run?

Does love get you excited and give you energy? Is that energy love?

For joy or fear we try to make it last

Are we afraid to be alone? so we continue to be in "love"

Try to put bad things in the past
Since love forgives all and is such a sought after gift

Can we forgive our partners if they do something wrong, do we need love that much? that we are willing to forgive anything.

But love is all we have so let's take care of it.
Like a drug you want to sustain
because when it's over you're left with pain

breakups can leave people in a bad state so we want to keep the high going just like a drug

it may take a toll on your body every time it fades away
often leaving you balding thinning or grey

love can often cause you to worry, but ultimately is this the price we are willing to pay for that feeling?

ALLURING FROM AFAR (WRITTEN 02.09.09)

I am the ship that sails on rough seas

so smoothly cutting through each wave silently.

Approaching so swift yet unseen

Much like an invisible beam

No alarms tripped or alerts sound

On the shores now made a mound.

In every type of weather I can be so tranquil on the outside

but you must look closer at the inside

for the energy required

to keep me so cute

is an in deafening audio you may want to press mute?

Engines stocked up pistons churning

the fire inside has not stopped burning

but stand back and admire from a distance how sleek I can appear
nothing to alert your audible ear

but take an inspection inside once,

once more and I cannot guarantee you won't go through that door

where engines were visible and gave such a lion's roar.

So all aboard because I'm off again

sailing seas by myself where it looks like I reign

ALLURING FROM AFAR

I am the ship that sails on rough seas

When you approach a potential partner you may perceive a hostile reception (rough seas) because you are not sure of the response you will get

so smoothly cutting through each wave silently.

We try to deflect any negative comments or moments that may happen and continue our pursuit of sharing common interest to get our desired goal

Approaching so swift yet unseen
Much like an invisible beam

Some people that are approached may not know a person's intentions but entertain their presence based on what they perceive the person intends

No alarms tripped or alerts sound

How love can often approach you without any fear

On the shores now made a mound.
Once you've introduced yourself you try to stay for as much time as possible without things going wrong
In every type of weather I can be so tranquil on the outside
but you must look closer at the inside

we can seem so calm or how we want to be perceived but inside we may be very nervous

for the energy required
to keep me so cute
is an in deafening audio you may want to press mute?

outside I may seem calm but inside my mind and body is going into overdrive

Engines stocked up pistons churning
the fire inside has not stopped burning

everything in your body is spurring you on and the fire (desire for love) is always there

but stand back and admire from a distance how sleek I can appear
nothing to alert your audible ear
but take an inspection inside once,

if a person would actual take a moment to assess the situation they may either see a genuine person or a trickster

once more and I cannot guarantee you won't go through that door
where engines were visible and gave such a lion's roar.

I am not sure of the response I would get and fear she might see through me that I am really nervous

So all aboard because I'm off again
sailing seas by myself where it looks like I reign

even if we have an unsuccessful approach to a potential partner we still have to keep our heads up and pretend we are ok and try again.

WHO'S THE VICTIM? (WRITTEN 16.09.09)

Can still feel the vile torments and rants in the air

I'm still wondering if this is about the colour of my skin and hair.

Repeating this word over again like I haven't heard it before,

he's clearly uneducated or maybe poor

I don't rise to his bait and give him the satisfaction

but don't think he knew how close I was just a fraction

to losing my calm and insulting him back

is his insults still just cause I'm black

I've dealt with this before wouldn't say it gets easier with time

this ranting and raving just wasting my time.

For what's the real issue becomes clear when you ask yourself how did I ever get here to being treated like a hated figure

this guy's still voicing off Nigg$r, Nigg$r

it's clear to see he has nothing more to add

probably this hatred is just extended from dad

because racists aren't born their raised

I thought this was all unacceptable these days.

I can't bare it I have to go

but this leaves me questioning what of tomorrow

would this guy ever get help and be saved

or forever be a victim whom no one can save.

What I heard in his voice so childish a fear

well this is so much more of a task.

again I ask how did we ever get here?

For the pain I feel is not for me but for his kind, who have little thought left of their own,

but have simply become a clone.

What are the real issues? here I'm left to ask

WHO'S THE VICTIM?

I can still feel the vile torments and rants in the air
I'm still wondering if this is about the colour of my skin and hair.

The hatred I felt was so much it made me question was it just about the colour of my skin

Repeating this word over again like I haven't heard it before,

Like a baby that has just learnt the word "no" they repeat it because they have learnt something new and get praise and encouragement for saying it

he's clearly uneducated or maybe poor

I could only perceive at the time he had issues of his own that lead him to want to hate someone so badly and make people feel inferior and how he felt

I don't rise to his bait and give him the satisfaction

I did not reply with any remarks that are racist but tried to insult him

but don't think he knew how close I was just a fraction
to losing my calm and insulting him back

I was really angry and did want to vent my anger by shouting at him

is his insults still just cause I'm black
I've dealt with this before wouldn't say it gets easier with time
this ranting and raving just wasting my time.

Their purpose seemed just to get a reaction from me but nothing else would have happened

For what's the real issue becomes clear when you ask yourself how did I ever get here
to being treated like a hated figure
this guy's still voicing off nigg$r, nigg$r

I thought about how a child would tease by repeating a word to annoy

it's clear to see he has nothing more to add
probably this hatred is just extended from dad

racists are not born they are made from an environment sometimes a family member or perhaps the television

because racists aren't born their raised
I thought this was all unacceptable these days.

With all the laws in the workplace against discrimination outside of the workplace it still is visible

I can't bare it I have to go
but this leaves me questioning what of tomorrow

I switched off the online game thinking who is this man going to abuse tomorrow?

would this guy ever get help and be saved
or forever be a victim whom no one can save.

Would anyone teach him not to hate for no reason or would he always be a victim of his own torment that makes him want to hurt others in response

What I heard in his voice so childish a fear
again I ask how did we ever get here.
For the pain I feel is not for me but for his kind, who have little thought left of their own,

His influences have been shaped by someone and they are living to please and get encouragement for what they perceive to be right and justified

but have simply become a clone.
What are the real issues? here I'm left to ask
well this is so much more of a task.

Finding out what was really wrong with this person may be too much to deal with because they may not believe they have a problem and ignorant to receive help

NEW ENERGY (WRITTEN 05.10.16)

It happens subconsciously all throughout the day

Like a bird after its prey

Could today be that day?

I don't want to cause any more delays

But it's hard when you been used to one way.

The outcome is pending but in my favour

Victory is almost here and something to savour

The battle was long but how did I beat such an equal foe?

My mind tells me yes but my heart tells me oh.

You have fought all the time in a particular manor

never focusing on the glitz and the glamour

but it's all there like spoils of war

the mindset has changed from being broke and poor.

So what do I do with this new found fame?

I don't know but this time I shall maintain,

a positive mind keep on doing what worked best

no need for more trials or tests

NEW ENERGY ANALYSIS

It happens subconsciously all throughout the day
Like a bird after its prey

Good things may occur throughout the day without us realizing how it came about just like how a bird naturally hunts it's pray

Could today be that day?
I don't want to cause any more delays
But it's hard when you been used to one way.

Something good has happened and you think our luck can change but you don't want to get too excited because you're not used to things going right for you

The outcome is pending but in my favor
Victory is almost here and something to savor

You're not sure but things seem to be going well, if you are successful you should try to hold onto it

The battle was long but how did I beat such an equal foe?
My mind tells me yes but my heart tells me oh.

You can't believe that you are finally having things go your way even though your head says yes enjoy it you know in your heart it won't last forever

You have fought all the time in a particular manor
never focusing on the glitz and the glamour

you have always been used to the position you was in but what do you do now that the unexpected has happened?

but it's all there like spoils of war
the mindset has changed from being broke and poor.

You can see a different way of living now that you couldn't see before

So what do I do with this new found fame?
I don't know but this time I shall maintain,

I am not sure how to proceed but I just try to carry on doing what worked

a positive mind keep on doing what worked best
no need for more trials or tests

you fear having to go through the same circumstances again when you had things in your favour

AGEING (WRITTEN 22.10.09)

Becoming older cartoons start to lose their interest

Less hair on the head more on the chest.

When young you would wish to be older

Now it's a big weight burden and you're colder

Appreciate things how they used to seem cheap

Now prices go up every week

Now the media say it's going to run out

But somehow your tax money can bail us out

give more and get less but we'll tell you it's better

you want the latest gadget just to feel better,

Spend all day long with this electronic demon

Saying your communicating but have lost your freedoms

But keep busy going nowhere

Sending your life through frequencies in the air

All designed for your comfort and ease

Don't kick up a fuss just keep typing please

Tell me your life minute by minute

Just an update in this police state

We'll watch you by camera know where you travel

sooner or later it will all unravel

AGEING

Becoming older cartoons start to lose their interest
Less hairs on the head more on the chest.

You've grown out of what used to keep you entertained
And are physically becoming older

When young you would wish to be older
Now it's a big weight burden and you're colder

It always seemed when you were young you had to wait to reach a certain age before
you could do certain things (drink, clubbing, drive).
Now you are older and it seems a burden because along with it comes bills and a lack of
energy

Appreciate things how they used to seem cheap
Now prices go up every week

Things always seem cheaper to buy (food, houses, cars) when you were younger but
then new taxes are introduced and prices seem to change all the time

Now the media say it's going to run out
But somehow your tax money can bail us out

We are taxed to help out causes when there is supposedly less of a thing so if it costs
more to buy we will use less but we still have the same need for the goods

give more and get less but we'll tell you it's better

goods are advertised as smaller but more convenient or with the same use

you want the latest gadget just to feel better,

people often buy goods to cheer themselves up as a comforter

Spend all day long with this electronic demon

We spend allot of time with either a TV or our mobile

Saying you're communicating but have lost your freedoms

People use the internet to express themselves so much but their freedom of speech can
often be scrutinized or critiqued by others whereas in a conversation in a person's
presence then you just get the audience you want to hear what you have to say

But keep busy going nowhere
Sending your life through frequencies in the air

We often feel we are achieving something by communicating over the internet or phone but we can achieve so much more by spending time with people giving body signals and letting people see our tone of voice so there is no misunderstanding like how there could be with text

All designed for your comfort and ease
Don't kick up a fuss just keep typing please
Tell me your life minute by minute

People write so much information about themselves letting everyone know where they are, what they're eating

Just an update in this police state
We'll watch you by camera know where you travel
sooner or later it will all unravel
cctv monitors us where ever we go but soon this can cause problems

MAKE IT (WRITTEN 30.03.10)

Born at a disadvantage because of the color of my

skin or does this make me more determined to win?

Things thrown your way you must deflect or gather up enough courage to

protect, what you have and what's rightfully yours no more fishing

around completing other people's choirs. But you work for me now don't

ask how just know that's the story now. Getting pretty busy can't get

complacent there's always someone younger and fresher as a

replacement. Stack while you can 'cause time flies by saving up just to
purchase a percent can't buy.

MAKE IT

Born at a disadvantage because of the color of my
skin or does this make me more determined to win?

*Sometimes feeling when things are against you can make you more determined
to succeed and prove people wrong*

Things thrown your way you must deflect or gather up enough courage to
protect, what you have and what's rightfully yours no more fishing
around completing other people's choirs.

*Sometimes other people try to give you their problems by telling you about it, you
sometimes have to concentrate on yourself and try to change the way you speak to
them.*

But you work for me now don't ask how just know that's the story now.
Getting pretty busy can't get

complacent there's always someone younger and fresher as a
replacement.

No one is un-replaceable there is always someone new and fresh with ideas

Stack while you can 'cause time flies by saving up just to
purchase a percent can't buy.

It's so hard to get on the property ladder compared to how it used to be

WHY SHOULD I? (WRITTEN 15.05.10)

Why should I have to compromise to work at my own demise seeing time and life slip before my eyes?

What you don't appreciate doesn't come your way but how to judge when it passes you by every day.

WHY SHOULD I? ANALYSIS

Why should I have to compromise to work at my own demise seeing time and life slip before my eyes?

We spend most of our life working not for ourselves or benefit but for others

What you don't appreciate doesn't come your way but how to judge when it passes you by every day.

Sometimes gratitude can be a very powerful thing bringing you things that you focus on and want, it's hard to tell how effective your desires can be.

ARE YOU NOT ENTERTAINED?

I want to be entertained

forget about the brain

Keep me preoccupied and keep me contained, in my cell that I enjoy I'll even pay you what a clever boy

just keep me busy with what I feel is important while you run over our rights and be extortionate.

Protect us from evil by taking away more for our good even spruce things up a bit in the hood.

But we never leave the cell not really, carry one in our pocket or view one at home see what time it starts keep quiet don't moan.

ARE YOU NOT ENTERTAINED?

I want to be entertained

as humans we seek entertainment in many forms from TV to our parents when we are babies

forget about the brain

normally we are not thinking about educating our self just our pleasure

Keep me preoccupied and keep me contained, in my cell that I enjoy I'll even pay you what a clever boy

We often pay high subscription prices to watch movies in our home to distract us from the realities and harshness of life

just keep me busy with what I feel is important while you run over our rights and be extortionate.

Usually laws go unnoticed or unannounced in the news when other stories are highlighted such as showbiz. Our food prices and gas keeps increasing regardless of the cost to produce.

Protect us from evil by taking away more for our good even spruce things up a bit in the hood.

Sometimes areas are renovated with new flats and shops to look good but the people that live there are often forced out by rent increases and are being moved out to more affordable areas, whilst richer people are moved in.

But we never leave the cell not really, carry one in our pocket or view one at home see what time it starts keep quiet don't moan.

Some people have become slaves to their phone with a location tracker letting companies know where they are all the time, finger scanning to know if it is you using the phone.

MY WORLD (WRITTEN 03.08.10)

I live in a world where everyone is in love but me, is this punishment or am I free, free from the phone calls that nag free from her worrying about what parts will sag.

I think she should just focus on getting a next bag, to carry around more things she won't use an excess amount of tissues.

I'm not a rapper but I do contain something sweet, talking below the waist but above the feet.

When I say these things I'm the creep when it's Mr. Muscles he is so deep, if I had lots cash would their attention change would I soon be considered all the range?

MY WORLD ANALYSIS

I live in a world where everyone is in love but me, is this punishment or am I free, free from the phone calls that nag free from her worrying about what parts will sag.

Sometimes it can seem like there are couples everywhere kissing and enjoying each other's company whilst we may be single. Sometimes what we perceive as a punishment (being single) can often be a blessing by us not having to argue about things or be obligated to do things like give reassurance.

I think she should just focus on getting a next bag, to carry around more things she won't use an excess amount of tissues.

Sometimes small things people enjoy can make a difference to people's perceptions about their partner.

I'm not a rapper but I do contain something sweet, talking below the waist but above the feet.

Whilst comparing myself to a sweet I give a reference to desires.

When I say these things I'm the creep when it's Mr. Muscles he is so deep, if I had lots cash would their attention change would I soon be considered all the range?

Often what I say because I am not muscly or seen as very handsome my views may seem dirty whilst others can say things and it is ok because they are a "charmer or man's man".

STATUS UPDATE (WRITTEN 10.10.10)

Put down the Facebook take the music out of your ears let's do something we haven't done in years

Communicate not through an electronic form of status update for peers

Let's use facial expressions who knows even tears. Where's the real emotion animals say more through twists and turns so why should we end up expressing our concerns through cold electric wires or satellite beams does anyone still have real dreams?

I'm barricaded by adverts all day long they try to get me to memorise their song. How many years can mankind cease to exist? Only concerned for the weekend to get pissed.

STATUS UPDATE ANALYSIS

Put down the Facebook take the music out of your ears let's do something we haven't done in years.

These days everyone seems concerned with communicating through their phones and showing how great their life is by taking pictures but it would often mean so much more to the people we are with to just enjoy the moment with them.

Communicate not through an electronic form of status updates for peers let's use facial expressions who knows even tears.

There is so much more that can be communicated with body language rather than typing text for people to try and figure out what you mean that can often be misinterpreted.

Where's the real emotion animals say more through twists and turns so why should we end up expressing our concerns through cold electric wires or satellite beams does anyone still have real dreams?

The animal king has allot of expressions that they use that humans don't. I question whether we still dream because we sit in bed on our phone doing things late into the night.

I'm barricaded by adverts all day long they try to get me to memorize their song.

Often what helps us remember products is the music that accompanies it

How many years can mankind cease to exist? Only concerned for the weekend to get pissed.
Is this really what people consider living? using technology to communicate without going out and consuming shows and ads for entertainment

IMAGINE (WRITTEN 26.11.10)

Imagine we didn't age we grew young

Imagine we had more than one sun

Time was given back to you to complete what was unfinished every second passed meant more of you replenished.

Would we still waste time on unimportant things walk around ideally considering things if you can imagine you're almost there if not sit down pull up a chair for the journey will begin when you're ready no more idealising the telly.

Can the mind take you places you don't want to go are you already there, you don't know.

You have gone back to the place you haven't been in a while even though you had a new style it's somehow different and doesn't satisfy it's like a bad thing you now ask why?

IMAGINE ANALYSIS

Imagine we didn't age we grew young

Would we still be concerned with pursuing our goals if we did not age?

Imagine we had more than one sun

With more than one sun would there be a night?

Time was given back to you to complete what was unfinished every second passed meant more of you replenished.

If we did get younger at some point would we try accomplish things we may not have done earlier

Would we still waste time on unimportant things walk around ideally considering things, if you can imagine you're almost there if not sit down pull up a chair for the journey will begin when you're ready no more idealising the telly.

Allot of the time we consider things rather than go ahead with them. If we can vision things then that is nearly enough to help us complete it because our mind is ready.

Can the mind take you places you don't want to go are you already there, you don't know.

Often what we think about the most whether bad or good is what comes to fruition because our energy is focused on it.

You have gone back to the place you haven't been in a while even though you had a new style it's somehow different and doesn't satisfy it's like a bad thing you now ask why?

Sometimes we know something or habit is bad for us and we think we are finished with it but we still go back to it because of bad habits.

POUNDING HEART (WRITTEN 19.07.11)

Deep inside and within your heart

Do not give up this is just the start

Of something bright it's not quite clear

But maybe this can be your year

Started off a slow race but finishing strong determined keep pace

Two things more that should be added to the list wouldn't that be fun wouldn't that be bliss. Don't count the days but someone will could be a big frill or go down like a chill.

Trying is better than not it's worth a go but let's see what I say tomorrow.

POUNDING HEART ANALYSIS

Deep inside and within your heart

Do not give up this is just the start

Sometimes we have to let our desires win and go for something in the moment
instead of waiting to see if we feel the same way the next day

Of something bright it's not quite clear
But maybe this can be your year

If you take an opportunity who knows where it could go

Started off a slow race but finishing strong determined keep pace

It may seem slow for you to achieve but you have to remain consistent to win like a
marathon

Two things more that should be added to the list wouldn't that be fun wouldn't
that be bliss. Don't count the days but someone will could be a big frill or go
down like a chill.

Do not pay attention to the time that passes although others will but things can go
either way negative or positive

Trying is better than not it's worth a go but let's see what I say tomorrow.

CHANGED THE GAME (WRITTEN 06.01.16)

You changed the game and the way we play haven't written a poem again until this day.

Wanted to tell people about you from the day we heard
had to keep it a secret three months how absurd.

The times coming close we're not ready yet needing to save and rearrange for you, how to act when you're here I haven't a clue.

But that's the fun we all go through, September it begins life starting a-new.

Fresh start I want better for you, looking after myself I now come in number two.

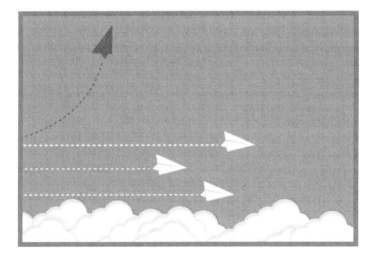

CHANGED THE GAME ANALYSIS

You changed the game and the way we play haven't written a poem again until this day.

Things have now changed where I am influenced again to write

Wanted to tell people about you from the day we heard
had to keep it a secret three months how absurd.

I wanted to tell people about my baby from the day I found out but it is bad luck to mention before three months so I did not

The times coming close we're not ready yet needing to save and rearrange for you, how to act when you're here I haven't a clue.

No one knows if they'll be ready with everything they need physically and mentally but we all try prepare.

But that's the fun we all go through, September it begins life starting a-new.
Fresh start I want better for you, looking after myself I now come in number two.

We always want better for our kids and place them in priority before us where as I always looked after myself first in every way.

WE

We enter this world through hope and faith

We submit to the norms that are there to "Protect and keep us safe"

We digest the cheaply made but cleverly placed all-encompassing food

We pay greatly to be entertained to take our minds off the daily dose of reality

We pay to stay in small boxes that are perceived to be owned by someone

We pay to be placed in our coop one on top another like we're in a supermarket

We pay for the product that pays for the ad that pays the millionaire to smile for the cameras

We won't do anything to change it but hit like and share because doing something requires the release of fear.

WE ANALYSIS

We enter this world through hope and faith

Our parents usually either hope for us to be conceived and have faith

We submit to the norms that are there to "Protect and keep us safe"

Any new laws that come out we are subjected to and cannot change

We digest the cheaply made but cleverly placed all-encompassing food

Unhealthy food options are everywhere but healthy food is rare and costs more

We pay greatly to be entertained to take our minds off the daily dose of reality

People pay large amounts for TV subscriptions and phones

We pay to stay in small boxes that are perceived to be owned by someone

People often believe the homes they buy in the western world are theirs but can easily be redeemed by banks or the govt. and the land is not owned

We pay to be placed in our coop one on top another like we're in a supermarket

We often pay large amounts for flats that sit one on top the other

We pay for the product that pays for the ad that pays the millionaire to smile for the cameras

The celebrity lifestyle we see is funded by our viewing and desire for it

We won't do anything to change it but hit like and share because doing something requires the release of fear.

Everyone talks how wrong it is on social media but does little to change the situation but announce how angry it makes them

CONTACT THE AUTHOR

Twitter- #Allusiveseeker

Blogger – Allusive seeker

Instagram- allusiveebooks

Printed in Great Britain
by Amazon

31413007R00029